PLAYING WITH FURY

LISA JACOB

Cover artwork design copyright © 2024 by Niki Lenhart
nikilen-designs.com

Published by Unruly Voices
unrulyvoices.com

ISBN 978-1-962538-79-4 (Trade Paperback)

FIRST EDITION

10 9 8 7 6 5 4 3 2 1

To BFF, whose life was my muse for three years while I wrote these poems.

To The Old Man, Waddles, and Mr. Pain in the Ass.

Contents

Introduction

I listened to a podcast about modern poetry: "Rhyming is bad." and "Forms are good."

I'm here to prove the former wrong, and the latter right.

Although I've written paranormal fiction for most of my life, I never sat down and wrote a lot of poetry. Because for the past two years, no novels have really come to mind or heart, I've realized that long forms of ideas are hard for me to keep up with.

Short forms, however, keep my attention. I picked up some poetry forms online and decided to play with them. With help from a rhyming dictionary (although some seemed forced) I was able to play with rhyme.

What you will see is some poems in all different forms.

I hope you enjoy the playful tails of cats and fury about modern life, using "normal" words that try not to stretch the imagination and make you work at understanding them.

Poetry is fun.

The Car Outside

HAIKU

A Mercedes-Benz
Waiting outside my window.
I feel paranoid.

Rumble-Shush

VILLANELLE

Max the ginger snores like a car.
He purrs as he breathes.
I hear him, no matter how far.

The center is his throat unmarred;
His ribs act like eaves
Max snores like a car.

I could bottle his whine in a jar,
To keep it safe from thieves;
I hear him, no matter how far.

His high snore, similar to a guitar,
Struck with wind and leaves.
But Max snores like a car.

The low rumble, a downshift in the ear,
A tree cracks without any leaves,
I still hear him, no matter how far.

The purrs he breathes always are
Audible as though he heaves—
My cat snores like a car
Forever I hear him, no matter how far.

My Mind

SESTINA

I have a brain full of worries,
Mental, physical, emotional.
Waiting for things to get hurt,
Things around me letting go,
People about me abandoning me,
The world being shitty in general.

I trust no one generally.
Because of them I have my worries
Depending on them bothers me.
It makes me feel, be too emotional
With money, I can't let go
Of the possibility of being hurt.

It's not unusual when I'm hurt,
Which happens monthly in general
As I bounce checks — off they go!
Money is the most of my worries.
I try not to let it make me emotional,
But always it goes round and round me.

My son's life and heart takes me
Because I don't want him hurt.
My arguments with him are emotional
Though it's about something else in general,
I give to him all my worries.
He can't let them go.

My dependence on others has to go,
I need to depend only on me,
What I have, not future worries,
Based on how I'll always hurt
To stop thinking about what is general
To ease up on the thoughts that are emotional.

My life has grown emotional—
My thoughts I can't let go
OCD—a thought of generals
Gathering to punish me
Because I deserve to be hurt
To fill my head with worries.

Full of emotion, I destroy me.
I try to go, but I keep getting hurt.
Unfortunately, my general thought is always worries.

Pounce!

FREE VERSE

UP! Goes the blanket.
The little lion sitting
On the dresser
Leaps through the air—
And flattens the fabric mountain.

HISS! Goes the lump
Underneath the blanket.
The little lion tracks
with his golden-slitted eyes
The hidden prey.

TWITCH! Goes the tail
Of the tiny golden lion.
He raises his rear and wiggles,
Ready…
Waiting…

OW! Yells the human
As the kitten's claws
Dig into the now-captured prey—
My hand.

Gratitude

SONNET

Bills are paid, finally, for once.
Thanking the gods with offerings
Of incense and gratitude using an ounce
Of Prosperity and assorted things—

Smoke wafting around the house,
A scent of cinnamon, saltpeter and wine—
The gods allow me to openly joust
With the charcoal and sandalwood divine

Offerings in my mind and by my hand
I ask for blessings from all the gods,
The ones who hear my petition and
Prayer, spells, on the path I trod.

Even my dearest, with Loki has done
In anger caused chaos; it's actually fun.

People Around Me

SESTINA

My friends are not really worthless,
A few have given me money
Without really working
For it, even though with BFF
I so badly want to murder,
Because of her inauthentic story.

Suddenly, she's got this story,
That I pretty much find worthless
In the sense of a murder
For her to give me money—
Oh, my dear BFF,
Get off your lazy ass and get to work.

My son has an issue about work
His own little story:
Taking care of me, not BFF,
Oh, no, never her. She's worthless.
Poor, destitute, less money,
Really meant to murder

The people who murder
My closed soul by making me work,
At a job that gives me little money,
Enough to continue my story.
About how worthless
I am, like BFF.

How I hate, dislike, the BFF.
That I don't care about and wish to murder,
By leaving her in her crap, worthless
To try and work
Her health is nothing compared to my story
Of how much money—

I spend way too much money.
"Preponderance of the Small" I Ching is BFF
Full of excuses and another story
To stop me from a murder,
Local on the stairs with work
To prove that she's worthless.

Give me money, I won't murder;
My BFF if she could only work,
Instead of coming up with a story
About how she is worthless.

It's All a Matter of Trust

FREE VERSE

I watch her deteriorate
Before my very eyes.
How toxic she's become—
Untrusting. Unbelieving.

It's all her fault,
Working at menial jobs,
Being loyal to a company
That doesn't care.

She saves her money,
But it's worthless now.
She's only as good
As an Uber.

Sleep til five in the afternoon.
I don't care anymore.
You didn't honor me,
Or our agreement.

Remains

FREE VERSE

You rode off into the sunset
On your brand-new motorcycle.
When I saw your remains,
There were flowers at your feet.

No marker remains of you
Except a box on my mantle,
And the grin of our son
When he's embarrassed.

It's been ten years now.
We've survived so long
Without your gentle laughter.
My leaden heart remains.

Sugar

VILLANELLE

After breakfast, my sugar goes high.
Only rice cereal, milk, and tea.
Took more than enough insulin to try

And make sure I'd have more by
Lunch. However, I do fear
I ate too much so my sugar is high.

Ever since Welch's fruit was a cheap buy,
I've eaten one, two, maybe three,
And took more insulin to try

To bring it down. Four hundred is still high.
I added Mounjaro which takes me
A long time while my sugar remains high.

In my food journal, I do lie
And I don't talk about being
That I took more insulin to try

To stop, but sensors don't lie
No matter what I eat
My sugar always goes too high
I keep taking more insulin to try and try.

Parting

HAIKU

I don't want to see
You anymore because you whine
Bitch and complain at me.

Little Books

RONDELL

Smaller than pockets, composition books
Of fifty tiny pages that just looks
Like something from a doll house,
About the size of a medium mouse
The first page contains the outlook.

Let it be known inside these books
Are short blurbs that are really hooks.
Something easy to read or browse,
Which may be in your wheelhouse—
Smaller than pockets.

Sewn into the sides of these books
The lines on the pages—gadzooks!
So tiny that a mere mouse
Could barely write within the space,
Smaller than pockets.

The Cat Muse

FREE VERSE

Waiting on the muse
I sit at the keyboard.
Fingers poised and ready.
Mind open and receptive.

I stare at the blank page,
My mind wanders.
Characters? Setting? Plot?
What to type next?

Then Tom, the wise old cat
Of my pride
Comes to tickle the ebony
Keys of the keyboard.

s43o056 F11
My screen explodes.
Tom lays across the keyboard.
F5 48957

I push him off,
he pushes back;
He is my muse today.

9/11 Air

SONNET

Breathing is yet a simple thing,
Controlled by a primordial mind;
Gently used for a song to sing
Endurance for this is hard to find.

Music surrounds the easy song
That take the air from the body.
Is it a song meant to mourn?
An expression of breath fully.

Wings carry you above the sky
To space, where we have tread.
The mourning dirge, by and by,
Fills the airwaves—a song for the dead.

Our fearless leader wanders confused on a stage,
While I wish New York would just turn the page.

Technology

SONNET

Press a button, it brings me to life
Swipe up, my screen goes bright.
Sometimes, though, I cause much strife
And then you show me all your might—

By pounding on the keyboard
Or calling tech support. Yelling in
Their ear; they tell you to abort
Control-Alt-Delete, a cardinal sin.

A soft reboot. Do not press start!
Unless it's a phone,
Then you must be smart
Hold the button down!

Eventually IT hangs up on you.
Stare at me! There's nothing you can do.

Sent Out to the World

FREE VERSE

For five years I have worked,
Slaved, bled, and cried;
Now, I send my baby,
Out into the world.

The world will see what beautiful prose
I have wrought. And Spielburg himself will call
To direct the motion picture,
And Brad Pitt will be the leading man.

I have visions of bestselling books.
I am number one on Amazon.
Everywhere.
I need to pick out a dress for the interviews.

Until...
I get my first one-star review.

I am crushed. The world has rejected
My baby, my most precious one,
That I paid to edit, and design, and lay out,
Shelling out half my paycheck.

No, this cannot be true!
It must be some mistake,
I tell the reviewer.
And then I start a war.

My name is dragged through the mud
Of Twitter, and Facebook,
And so much social media
I am a failure.

Or maybe, only this book
Was not what I had dreamed.
It's time to practice
Having another baby.

Toxic

SONNET

I don't have any more care to give.
Not to you, my bestie old friend.
I have my own life to live,
It's now too close to the end.

My life is too short to deal with you,
Your nagging, complaining and judgment.
I beg for others to rescue
Me with their encouragement.

You need a better hobby,
Than pontificating from on high.
I have had it with your snobby
Attitude, and heavy sighs.

Please, just go away
Immediately and without delay.

Garbage

PANTOUN

We fill our bins
With refuse and detritus
Of our lives,
Packaging no longer needed.

With refuse and detritus,
We show to the garbage men
Packaging no longer needed,
Covered in plastic smelly bags.

We show to the garbage men
As they see the bags explode in the truck
Covered in plastic smelly bags
A gathering of the neighborhood.

As they see the bags explode in the truck
Of our lives,
A gathering of the neighborhood—
We fill our bins.

Beliefs

VILLANELLE

There are so many statues in my house.
Visages of gods and goddesses in my heart alive
With incense daily I do douse.

Horus, wearing Ra or Aten the sun disk,
Falcon-headed son of the god revived,
There are Egyptian statues in my house.

Fleet-footed messenger Hermes,
My patron in knowledge by scribes,
With air and incense I do douse.

Another Greek goddess, Athena, arouse
Within prayers that do not deprive
My Greek statues in my house.

Apollo, sun-god, similar to Horus,
My other patron of arts, arrive!
With incense and offerings I do douse.

Lastly, a happy Buddha on my desk,
What will they think when I die?
There are so many gods in my house,
With prayer and requests I do douse.

Dreary

SONNET

Good morning, as I find the rain,
Spattering against my glass window
Although the tropical storm's main
Eye is south, it shows the intro

Of Ophelia's stormy wings,
That hit the Carolinas and Virginia
With rain and pummeling wind.
It's now broken up due to inertia.

Landfall makes the entire storm light,
By the time it comes northeast
It has turned gentle and bright.
The rain, however, has been released.

I enjoy these days of overcast,
It will go away much too fast.

Blob

FREE VERSE

Released from his assholeness,
Oh, so happy, we celebrate!
Blob is his nickname
Even though he was more than an idiot.
Really, he treated her like shit, but!
That's what I do.

Undependable

PONTOUN

I call her, begging
I swallow my pride
Then she gives me the lecture:
"Can you afford it?"

I swallow my pride.
"Will you have enough?"
"Can you afford it?"
"Will you pay it?"

"Will you have enough?"
Unsaid because of lack of trust:
"Will you pay it…"
Back to me.

Unsaid because of trust—
You are undependable.
Always to me
Your words in your mouth.

You are undependable
Then she gives me the lecture,
Your words in my mouth.
I swallow my pride.

Nature

SONNET

Nature scares me with bugs
Dying or dead trees,
The cycle of life with slugs
A flower covered in bees...

The river below rushes at my feet,
Carrying leaves away,
Flowing down under the street,
Along with it decay;

This is what scares me, the end.
Squishy and cloying and clinging
Webs and worms and things that blend
Frogs, their beady eyes bleeding—

The woods don't calm me.
But frightens like the wild sea.

Cat in a Window

HAIKU

Krimson is lying down
In a space made just for him,
His tail tucked away, stuck.

Prime-Time Media

FREE VERSE

They used to call it Fake News
But it's really "informed opinions".

Listen to the false grey-hair,
The salt and pepper person,
The guy with glasses,
The young guy at eight,
The old guy who can't say adjectives,
Because his hero can't communicate.

The Hero comes up with bull
And they clean it up or make it happen.
Good people are racist, on both sides.

All the media is white at night.

Ode to a Sleeping Cat

FREE VERSE

Curled into a half-ball,
Legs stretched out for distance,
Establishing territory, including all
Of the couch, allowing no entrance.

His purr rises and falls in silence,
He snores with a tiny "meu"
In his sleep, he stretches one leg out
Attacking prey, but only a few.
On his tiny paws, a sense of balance
Birds in his dream all tense,
Make him ruffle his coat.

Fall Spices

SESTINA

The air is crisp with a bite to it.
Fog fills the early morning air
As I drive to my newest occupation;
Six hours wasted, sitting in a chair,
While I watch the tree's leaves fall.
That is the name of the season.

I take coffee with pumpkin spice seasoning.
The sweetness is far too much for it.
Extra cream, no sugar, it falls
To the ground, spreading over the air
As I knock the sweet drink from my chair
Distracted by its occupation.

Sweetness is filled with an occupation
Of pumpkin spice latte this season
I sit alone inside with the chairs
Another person then orders it—
Do you realize that in the air
The latte is sweetened so much this fall!

I go to a different shop, looking for the fall
Spice that is its only occupation
Clove and pumpkin, scenting the air
Its only note for this season
To make brown eyes blue, it's
The wrong spice in this chair.

So, I go home, sit in my chair,
I write this while dozing—I fall
To the desk. I jerk awake, it
Finally catching up, this lack of occupation.
The dreariness of this fall season
Fills my limited air.

The house has a perfumed air.
I get up slowly from my chair,
Stumble to the oils, to pick one for the season.
"Autumn Air" is meant for this fall.
No clove, but orange is its fall occupation.
I add some more clove to it.

Now the air, not coffee, falls,
I go back to my chair to make my occupation
Of this season to replicate it.

Where the Story Goes

ROUNDEL

The muse takes me for a ride.
I expected humor, remarks that were snide,
I wanted Thalia, comedy muse;
Instead, Melpomene, tragic muse.
A murder mystery, definitely my pride

And joy, in the genre I do thrive,
Someone always in my stories dies,
Because I have been bruised
By hate, anger, and fury let loose.
My muse takes me.

A romance, I have tried,
With a happy, satisfied bride.
But my dark muse does refuse
To accept love and happiness true,
So along I go with this midnight guide,
The muse takes me.

On Breakfast

ANACRENONTEA

I have a list of only breakfast food
It all depends on what's my mood.
Typically, I have cereal and milk,
Tea for caffiene, or more of that ilk
I would love something from a diner;
Close by, yes, nothing finer.

I replicate the diner experience at home—
But I can't seem to copy it, even with cooking tomes,
It's the home fries that are hardest,
Duplicating all of the spices.
Eggs should be fluffy, bacon crisp and well-done
Breakfast, to be honest, to make is not fun.

Outside Smokers

VILLANELLE

I hear the radio outside, tinny—
Needs bass, but the smoker doesn't care
He inhales, his body really skinny.

The air out here is not at all windy,
Flicking away the blunt with a flare,
The radio he plays is overly tinny.

His clothes, to me, are old and dingy.
He looks across the street at me with a glare,
He inhales, his body really skinny.

Fills his longs, showing his chest thinly,
He waits for another to dare
Join the radio playing tinny

Songs. Here she comes, sickly
And thin. Skin so fair.
They inhale, their bodies very skinny.

Her took to me is fishy,
Smoke anything, I don't care.
The radio continues the tinny
Noise; she exhales, her body skinny.

Misery

FREE VERSE

He comes to me, jaw tightly clenched
Fury, anger—
Or stress over many problems

Which are all my fault.
Involving
Him to make misery spread.

That is the point of it all…
Loneliness
No other one in the house—

But a child.

About the Author

Lisa Jacob has been writing since she could hold a pencil and draw a straight line. She wrote fan fiction before branching out into novels and short stories.

In the early 2000's, Lisa was a carny in a traveling circus for a summer, where she met her husband. Interested in magic(k), cards, and divination, she lives in Rhode Island with her son and cats.

Lisa is also the author of *Carnival Farm*, *Real Magic for Writers*, and the "Grimaulkin" and "War Mage" fantasy series.

You can find out more about Lisa Jacob at her website, lajacob.com.

Also By the Author

CARNIVAL FARM

by Lisa Jacob

When a local veterinarian decides to take over a traveling carnival's petting zoo, she doesn't realize the insanity behind the scenes.

Available from Paper Angel Press in hardcover, trade paperback, digital, and audio editions

paperangelpress.com

REAL MAGIC FOR WRITERS

by Lisa Jacob

Magic is real.
It also helps with writing.

Available from Unruly Voices in trade paperback and digital editions

unrulyvoices.com

You Might Also Enjoy

How do you spell the sound of crickets

by Paolo Bruni & Jory Post

"Write to me. Keep me alive," wrote Jory Post to Paola Bruni as he was dying of inoperable cancer.

how do you spell
the sound of crickets

Paola Bruni & Jory Post

ARTISANAL GIBBERISH

by Matthew Legare

Munificent musings on multiple matters, mainly manifesting in a literary litany of alliterative madness. It's poetry, if you squint...

Available from Unruly Voices in trade paperback and digital editions

unrulyvoices.com

Milton Keynes UK
Ingram Content Group UK Ltd.
UKHW022336230424
441619UK00015B/795